Bite Sized Specifics

Blues Piano

Walking-Bass

Southern House Publishing

ISBN: 978-1-9196118-9-1

tylermusic.co.uk

CONTENTS

Introduction

The idea of this book - or indeed this series - is rather than having the usual single book that skims over an entire broad subject that perhaps never goes into quite enough detail, we would instead split the project into different subjects with each book covering a different aspect of playing blues piano. The idea being that a separate book could hopefully be more detailed than those that cover everything. A basic level of piano playing is obviously required, and I would suggest a general grounding in the style before this series.

There are quite a few variations in blues piano styles, but a common form of left-hand is without doubt the walking style, or the walking-bass. This is not only a piano thing of course as the bass guitar or double bass also commonly use this form, but this is specifically a look at how play it on the piano.

What is a walking-bass? It's simply a form of playing that earned its name by the way it kind of walks up and down the instrument. It moves up and sometimes down the keyboard (on piano that is) which makes the name fit perfectly.

Being that we are dealing with the left-hand here, the book concentrates on that rather than complicating matters further. In order to play this style you really need to have complete independence between the two hands, therefore it's important to practice the left-hand separately to begin with until it becomes internalised and requiring little thought, ideally you want it to be almost automatic.

The context of this is directed more towards what you might call a slow blues, not that it has to be limited to this, but the walking style is more commonly used on slower pieces, this is a generalization though, as it can also be heard/used at a faster pace.

The book will cover the very basics, going over how the bass patterns are constructed, which notes are used and the scales that they're from. It looks at different fingering ideas, different positions/ranges, target notes and passing notes. It looks at chord changes, covers various patterns and has twelve-bar blues progression examples in different keys to use as practice. All this will hopefully help give you a basis from which to develop your blues piano playing.

Important Notes

Left-Hand Only

Being that we are dealing with the left-hand on the piano here, the book will concentrate on that, with the exception of a few ideas of how to begin practising with the right-hand. In order to play this style you really need to have complete independence between the two hands, as the left-hand needs to be able to play along doing its thing while you concentrate more on improvising with the right-hand. With that in mind it's important to practice the left-hand separately to begin with, at least until it becomes internalised and requiring as little thought as possible (for a basic pattern at least).

Triplet Timing

The music here will primarily consist of quarter notes (or crotchets if you prefer) giving a single note per beat of music. When the music deviates from this it will do so with a triplet/shuffle feel, which is the standard feel with blues. So it's important to remember that all eighth notes (quavers) are played with a triplet feel.

This point is vital, and I can't stress this enough. The sign that denotes this (shown below) will be seen throughout the book as a reminder.

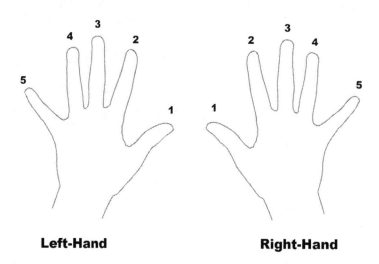

Fingering Suggestions

You may or may not be interested in fingering ideas for the walking-bass, it's certainly not vital to begin with, but it will be covered from page.54. The standard form of finger numbering will be used as shown below.

Left-Hand   **Right-Hand**

Basic Chord Progressions

These are examples of some traditional blues chord progressions, all these use the typical twelve-bar format which is the basis of traditional blues music and so will be used throughout the book. There will be some more complex variations included later on in the book, as not all blues follows the standard progressions.

Progression No. 1

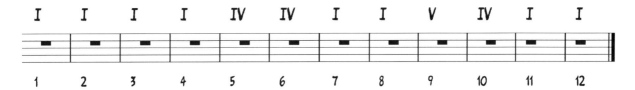

Progression No. 2

Progression No. 3

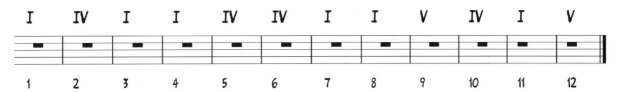

Progression No. 4

Walking Bass-Lines

One of the interesting things about playing with walking-bass patterns is that pretty much any note is useable, as long as it fits the context of the music. Now that doesn't mean you can randomly play anything and it will work, but it is a very open style of playing.

Basic Major Scale

Above you have the major scale in the key of 'C'. I must point out that it will help greatly to be familiar with the major scales, if not then I'd recommended a quick brush up before continuing. Now while you can use every note of the major scale at some point, there are a set of notes within it that can be considered the basic go to notes, the backbone of any pattern really.

Main Go To Notes

The basic notes consist of the keynote (root) the third, fifth and sixth, plus you could include the root note one octave up, although that is a repeat. These four notes are no surprise as the first three notes form a major chord and the additional sixth creates a major-sixth chord, all fairly standard.

With these four notes alone you can create walking-bass patterns that are the common basic pattern that everything else really stems from. So before we complicate matters, let's have a look at some ideas of how we can use these to create bass-lines for the left-hand on the piano.

Walking Pattern 1

To begin with we can play a simple pattern created from a major chord. In the example below we're on a 'C' chord and will begin with the root note that moves to the third, then the fifth and then back down to the third. Each note is played on the beat for a whole beat.

Triad Pattern

Practice this over the twelve-bar progression below, the pattern remains the same for each of the chords with the notes all based off the relevant chord. The chord progression is a simple one, as is the bass pattern itself, but when played, try not to play the notes robotically. Rather, try to 'feel' the music as you go along, by getting into the groove so to speak (Even though it is basic to begin with). Blues is all about the feel of the music, complicated or simple, when played well it conveys a degree of emotion. For this to work I'd recommended playing along to a blues drum backing (as per audio download) and try to imagine you're playing a double bass in a dark smokey club or something similar (optional of course).

12-Bar Practice. 1

1 AUDIO

Walking Pattern 2

Now it's time we added another note to the pattern, namely the sixth. This works extremely well, adding interest to the bass-line as it moves away from the major chord tones. Here it is essentially being used by itself, but it also works well as a lead up to another note which we will add next time.

Starting with the root (the common starting point) we move up through the third, fifth, and the sixth (which replaces the repeated third in the previous pattern).

Triad Pattern With Added Sixth

You will notice that this time the twelve-bar progression has been changed, with the second bar now being the 'IV' chord. Again, it's best to practice it to a blues drum backing in order to get the feel of the music as you play, ideally anyway, but a metronome is always a good idea.

12-Bar Practice. 2

2 ◀ AUDIO

One of the great things about the walking-bass is that it never appears to be static, it always seems to be changing which is more interesting than a repetitive one bar pattern. So taking that idea, we can take the two patterns that have already been covered and combine them in different ways.

Combination One

3 AUDIO

Combination Two

4 AUDIO

The second version is essentially a mirrored copy, swapping out pattern one where pattern two was and vice versa. This begins to show how versatile the style can be.

Walking Pattern 3

Next in-line to look at would be a pattern with an additional root note added an octave up from the starting point. With this now included you are covering a more complete range of motion, although the bass can obviously stretch over more than one octave, but that will come later.

Starting with the root note, we move up through the third, fifth, sixth and then the octave root. From here we move back down through the same notes, going in reverse order with the sixth, fifth, and third. From this end point we are set nicely to go back to the root for the next bar, whether that's the same chord or not.

Two Bar Pattern (Octave To Octave)

Notice on the twelve-bar example below that the second bar is now a 'C' (the 'I' chord) as the pattern needs two bars to develop fully. For this same reason bars nine and ten use a shorter pattern ending with the sixth, as there's only one bar of each chord which isn't enough for the full octave pattern.

12-Bar Practice

5 AUDIO

Here we have two example twelve-bar progressions that use the octave to octave two bar pattern. The progressions are slightly different as are the patterns used within them at various points. All of them are from what has been covered so far.

Combination One

6 ◀ AUDIO

Combination Two

7 ◀ AUDIO

The second combination has a chord change on bar two, so the first two bars use a shorter pattern. Most of the other bars have been swapped over compared to example combination one.

Walking Pattern 4

Next we shall add the flat-seventh to the available notes (dominant/minor seventh) which adds some extra interest to the sound.

This is another two bar pattern, starting with the root note we move up through the third, fifth, sixth and finally the flat-seventh. From here we move back through the same notes in reverse order and finish on the third.

Two Bar Pattern (Including Seventh)

Seeing as this is a two bar pattern, we keep the 'I' chord for the first two bars. Bars nine and ten naturally use a shorter pattern, which happens to be the first bar of the pattern above.

12-Bar Practice

Here are twelve-bar examples that include the two-bar seventh pattern along with the three previous patterns, all combined in different orders. They are for the most part mirror images of each-other where the seventh pattern on one will have an alternative pattern on the other.

Combination One

Combination Two

If the second bar in the progression happened to be the 'IV' chord, then naturally a shorter version would be applied for bars one and two.

Walking Pattern 5

Moving back to a single bar pattern, instead of playing a single note per beat (crotchet/quarter notes) here we introduce a couple of eighth notes/quavers. Bear in mind that these will be played using a triplet feel, as the sign denotes.

This still uses the same notes as previously, starting with the root note we move up through the third, fifth and sixth, where it drops back down to the fifth.

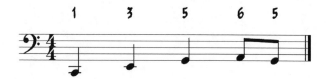

One Bar Pattern (With Quavers/Eighth Notes)

Seeing as this is a single bar pattern we had the option of using a 'IV' chord for the second bar. All subsequent bars can use the same pattern if so desired, which for the sake of a first time practice we have done below.

12-Bar Practice

12

Here are twelve-bar examples that include the two-bar seventh pattern along with a selection of the previous patterns mixed in.

Combination One

12 AUDIO

Combination Two

13 AUDIO

Walking Pattern 6

Time to add another note to the mix, this time we are adding the minor-third. Being more of a passing note than a target note, here it is used just before the third, stepping from one to the other and resolving the dissonance of the minor.

Starting with the root note we move up through the third and fifth, from here it drops back down to the minor third and third.

One Bar Pattern (With Minor Third)

12-Bar Practice

14 ◀ AUDIO

From the example on the last page you might have noticed an important aspect of the walking bass style, it happens at the chord changes between 'C' and 'F' on bars one/two and four/five. The last note of the first chord leads seamlessly into the root note of the next chord, the two notes being only a semi-tone apart. I refer to this as a leading note as it leads into the next chord.

Walking pattern number six probably isn't something you would play continuously throughout like the first practice example. Instead, it'll be added here and there to mix things up, that's not to say you couldn't use it all the way through of course.

Leading Notes

The last example mentioned a note that leads into the chord change. When I refer to a leading note like this I'm talking about the last note (or two) of one chord leading into the next chord. The idea of these is to have a clean transition between chords and it's an intrinsic part walking a bass. It enables the chord change to be easy and smooth due to the small movement required.

Example No. 1

The flat-fifth of the 'C' chord steps nicely up to the root of the 'G' chord.

Example No. 2

The flat-fifth of the 'C' chord steps down to the root of the 'F' chord.

Example No. 3

The third of the 'C' chord steps up to the root of the 'F' chord.

Example No. 4

The sixth of the 'G' chord steps up to the root of the 'F' chord.

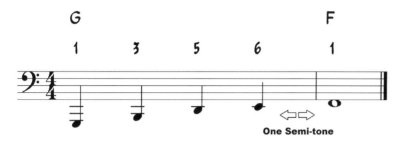

Example No. 5

The flat-sixth of the 'C' chord steps down to the root of the 'G' chord.

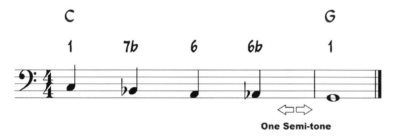

Example No. 6

The flat-fifth of the 'F' chord steps up to the root of the 'C' chord.

Walking Pattern 7

Adding the Flat-Fifth

Time to add another note to the tool box, this time it's the flat-fifth. This is really useful as it sits directly between the fourth and fifth, making it ideal for the transition to either the 'IV' chord or the 'V'.

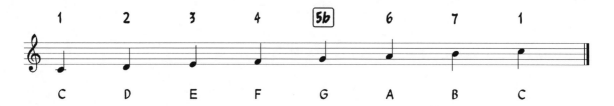

Two Bar Pattern (With Flat-Fifth)

This starts on the root note and moves through the third, fourth, flat-fifth and fifth, before moving back down through the fourth, third, and second. Obviously being a two bar pattern this can only be used in certain places, but here we have a twelve-bar progression that uses no less than two bars of each chord, retaining the 'V' chord on bar ten.

12-Bar Practice.

17 AUDIO

18

Walking Pattern 8

Taking the previous pattern a little further, here we continue to walk up through the second bar. This incorporates the flat-seventh and a note we haven't used yet which is the major-seventh (a passing note).

Two Bar Pattern Walking Up

This starts on the root note and moves through the third, fourth, flat-fifth, fifth, sixth, flat-seventh and seventh. This could be used at any point where a chord is used for two whole bars, but it doesn't really work properly if repeated twice on the same chord. Below it isn't used on the first two bars.

12-Bar Practice

18 ◀ AUDIO

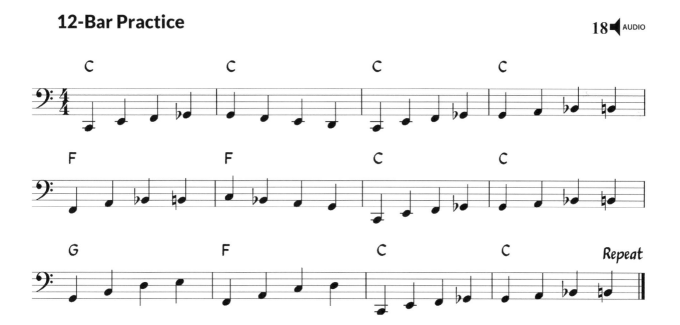

You may have noticed that ending on the major seventh (which here should be considered a passing note) makes it sound like it could continue on further, which of course it can, so next we will do just that.

Walking Pattern 9

Now we are really walking, moving two bars upwards and then two bars down. Below are two examples that extend the previous pattern further.

Two Bars Up Two Bars Down No.1

Two Bars Up Two Bars Down No.2

Both versions walk down from the seventh to the second, but the first version does this via the flat-sixth, where the second version uses the flat-fifth instead, along with the flat-third on the end.

12-Bar Practice

19 AUDIO

This pattern requires four bars to develop so can only be used here on the first four bars, to use it anywhere else would require it to be modified somewhat.

Walking Pattern 10

So far we have looked at walking patterns that are quite linear, but they don't have to be quite so ordered. Here we will look at some patterns where you have a small jump across the keyboard rather than only stepping up by a semi-tone or tone.

One To Seven Walk-Down Pattern

Here we start on the root as usual, but instead of walking up gradually we now jump right up to the flat-seventh. From here we return to the more usual gradual walk as it moves down (mostly chromatically) through the sixth, flat-sixth, fifth, flat-fifth, fourth and finishing on the flat-third.

12-Bar Practice

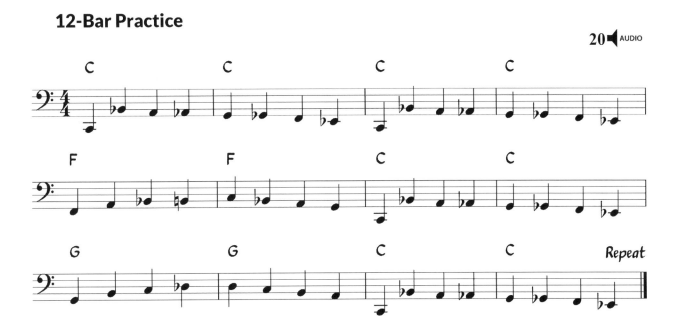

Pattern 10 Variations

Below is a repeat of the pattern we looked at on the previous page.

Now part of the enjoyable thing of the walking bass is the ability to alter it as you play, nothing is set in stone. So taking this pattern we can have a play around with it and alter it in different ways. None of these changes are huge as it still retains the basis of what it began with, we are just changing or adding the odd note here and there.

Variation No. 1

Here the last beat has been divided into two notes, with the flat-third moving to the third.

Variation No. 2

Here the first beat has the root note played twice instead of once.

Variation No. 3

Here the second beat now plays the flat-seventh twice.

Variation No. 4

This version is the same as the original except the last beat is divided into two and drops down to the second.

Variation No. 5

On this version, after jumping up to the flat-seventh it immediately drops back to the root note for a moment before returning to the original path. This retains the altered last beat.

Variation No. 6

Here the root note is played twice before using the same jump up and down as the previous variation.

Variation No. 7

This time the sixth is repeated twice and the fourth repeated twice, it then drops to the second for the last note.

Variation No. 8

Here the second beat is divided and moves from the sixth to the flat-seventh, adding a semi-tone step up which then immediately steps back down again.

Variation No. 9

This does a similar thing to variation eight, but this time it's on beat two of the second bar, stepping up from the fourth to the flat-fifth and back down again.

Variation No. 10

This is the same as the first pattern until the end, the last two beats each have two notes where we drop briefly down to the root note before using a familiar flat-third to third movement.

Note that this is ideal for moving to the 'IV' chord, as the third is a semi-tone step from the root note of that chord, making a nice smooth seamless transition.

Several twelve-bar progressions for practise with different combinations of the patterns looked at over the last few pages.

Combination One

21 AUDIO

Combination Two

22 AUDIO

Combination Three

Combination Four

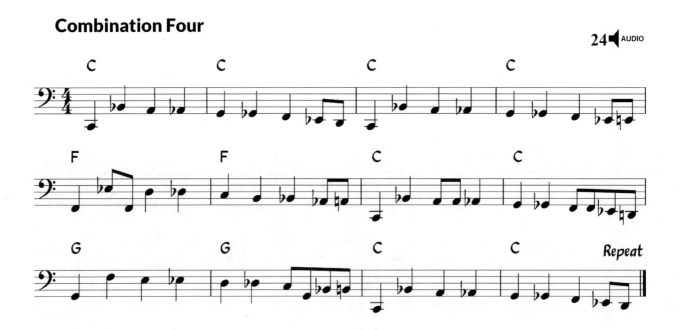

26

Changing Direction

At chord changes when you play the root note of the new chord, rather than jumping down for the next root note it's possible to use new root note an octave higher and from there walk down instead of up.

Below we have two examples taken from a twelve-bar progression, these are 'IV' to 'I' chord changes. The first drops down an octave or so to hit the root note, the second version drops down a single tone to the root note. Both are equally valid, but the second is clearly a much smoother transition than the first.

Dropping An Octave

Remaining Above

Variation No. 1

Here it simply drops chromatically from the sixth to the flat-sixth of the 'F' chord which is only a semi-tone from the root note of the 'C' chord.

Variation No. 2

Using the same timing, on the end of the 'F' chord use the fourth and flat-fifth. This has the 'F' chord ending only a semi-tone lower than the root note of the 'C' chord.

Combination One

25 AUDIO

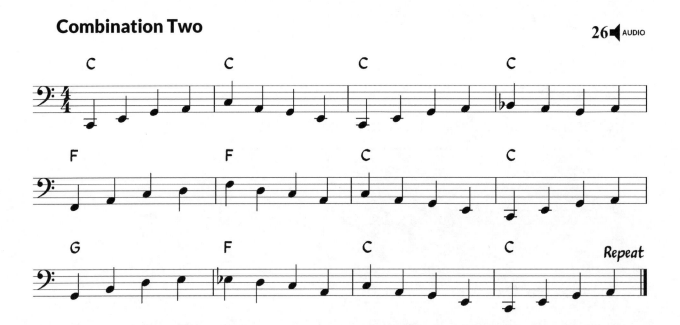

Combination Two

26 AUDIO

Starting Downwards

It's common place to start a walking-bass pattern by moving in an upwards direction, in-fact it's what you nearly always see/hear, but you can of course start by moving downwards if it fits with the music.

Down Over One Bar

Moving down over one bar using the root, flat-seventh, sixth and fifth. This could be repeated over and over, or be extended as per the next example.

Down Over Two Bars

This begins the same but then continues on further, using the fourth, third, second and then ending on the root.

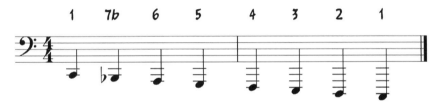

Combination One

27 AUDIO

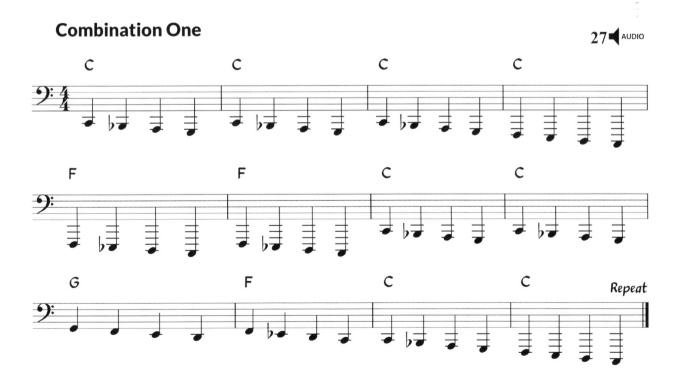

29

Alternative Options

Example No. 1

A quick change of direction at the chord change.

Example No. 2

A slight drop from the sixth to the third to set up for the chord change.

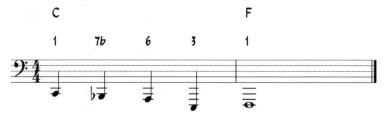

Example No. 3

Another drop down to then walk up, being a slightly more involved set up for the chord change of the following bar.

Example No. 4

Jumping up an octave at the root note allows for an easy change of the range you're playing in by moving an octave instantly.

Example No. 5

Combining a set-up for the chord change with an octave jump at the root note of the following chord in the second bar.

Example No. 6

A different combination of notes are used here, moving mostly chromatically from the flat-seventh down to the fourth where it drops to the flat-third.

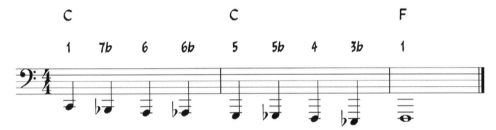

Combination Two

28 AUDIO

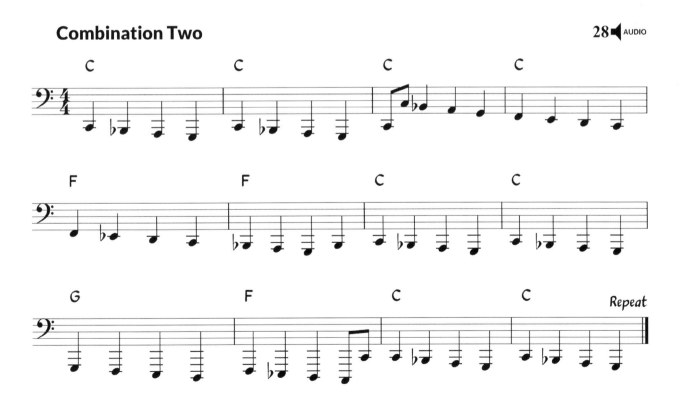

Combination Three

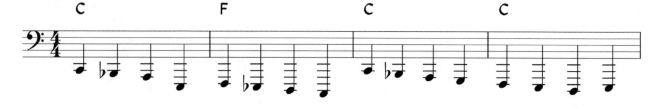

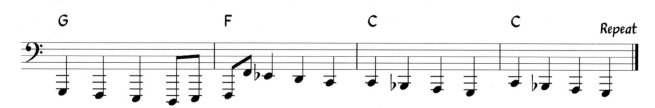

Combination Four

Further On Up

So far we have remained within a relatively small range of motion, keeping each pattern per chord within an octave range, but there is no reason why you can't extend this range. This isn't necessarily something you'd do all the time, but you can add it in places to make things more interesting. For the majority of the time you would tend to keep the bass range a little more restrained, but on the odd occasion or on certain songs where it will work/fit in, it's fun to move around further.

Example No. 1

Here the 'C' chord is taken up past an octave range, hitting the root note two octaves up before moving back down again.

Example No. 2

This starts on the root of the 'C' chord and moves up past the octave, switching to a downwards movement after reaching the flat-seventh.

Example No. 3

On the 'C' chord we move up to the root octave, but instead of moving back down it continues on until reaching the root of the next chord.

Example No. 4

Here the 'C' chord walks up past the root and onto the fifth, from there it drops down to the flat-fifth and then nicely down to the root of the next chord

Example No. 5

Here it walks down from the root note, past the octave point and down to a third which leaves it a semi-tone from the root of the next chord.

Example No. 6

Starting on the root of the C' chord, move down past the lower root and then use the flat-seventh, sixth and fifth, which lead nicely to the root of the 'F' chord.

Example No. 7

This starts on the root 'G' and moves up past the octave root and through the second, flat-third and third, which leads to the root of the next chord 'C'.

Short Walk

This pattern is relatively short in range as it only moves up to the fifth before returning back down again.

Short Walk To Fifth

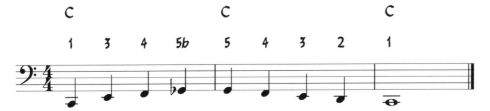

This pattern starts on the root and moves up chromatically through the third, fourth, flat-fifth and fifth. At this point it walks down (missing the flat-fifth) through the fourth, third, and second.

The example above shows the pattern ending on the root in the third bar, this has the pattern ending, but this note could instead be the start of a repeat of the pattern or alternatively a change of chord.

Repeating Same Pattern

Same Pattern To Different Chord

Variations

There's ways you could vary this pattern, but then the beauty of a walking bass is that it is fluid and open to change, you can move up or down, repeat sections, go slow or fast or jump up or down to something new. Over the page are a few examples of ways that this particular one could be altered. The more busy it becomes the less often you would use it in reality.

Variation No. 1

This adds a brief drop down to the third on the end of the first bar. The third does sound a little out of place after the flat-fifth, but it works as a passing note.

Variation No. 2

Here the pattern has you drop briefly down to the root note after the fifth is played in the second bar

Variation No. 3

This is similar to variation number two, but here the drop to the root note is after the flat-fifth on the first bar.

Variation No. 4

Here we combine variations one and two, dropping back to the third and root respectively.

Variation No. 5

Following with the same theme, the root is added twice in the first bar after the fourth and flat-fifth, making a chopping motion.

Variation No. 6

Adding to variation number five by adding the root after the fourth on bar two.

Variation No. 7

Adding to variation five with the root note after the fifth on the second bar.

Variation No. 8

Here the root note is added twice on both bars. With this many root notes added the alternating back and forward motion makes it more like a boogie-woogie type bass pattern than a slow blues, but music styles often blend and cross-over.

Variation No. 9

Doubling up with the root note on the first beat and dropping back to the root once on beat two, after that it's the standard pattern.

Variation No. 10

This adds the flat-third on the second beat of bar one before moving to the third

Variation No. 11

On the second bar after reaching the fifth, drop down to the third and move chromatically through the fourth and flat-fifth.

Variation No. 12

This is a slight alteration on variation eleven, where the flat-fifth on the last beat of bar two is replaced by the fifth. This is less dissonant than the flat-fifth, but will change where you can walk to next in some circumstances.

More Chord Transitions

Mentioned briefly earlier on, here we'll examine how some of the previous patterns can be used to transition between chords.

'C' To 'G' Transition

This pattern is perfect for moving from the 'I' chord to the 'V' chord ('C' and 'G'). The last note on the 'C' chord is one semi-tone below the root of the 'G' making it a seamless step.

'C' To 'F' Transition

Here it's moving from the 'I' chord to the 'IV' chord ('C' and 'F'). The last note on the 'C' chord is one semi-tone above the root of the 'F'.

'F' To 'C' Transition

Here it's moving from the 'IV' chord to the 'I' chord ('F' and 'C'). The last note on the 'F' chord is one semi-tone below the root of the 'C'.

'G' To 'C' Transition

Now moving from the 'V' chord to the 'I' chord ('G' and 'C'). The last note on the 'G' chord is one tone above the root of the 'C'.

Combination One

Combination Two

Combination Three

Combination Four

Dropping Mid-Way

Rather than just moving up or down in a linear fashion, you can also drop down midway through a pattern. This kind of splitting of the pattern really breaks things up and makes it more interesting, not just to listen to but also to play.

Example No. 1

On the 'C' chord below you can see how it walks up but then drops a semi-tone, ending the bar a semi-tone away from the root note of the next chord. After this transition to the next chord, instead of walking upwards it drops down to the third. There's nothing unusual about following the root with the third, but this time the third is an octave lower.

Example No. 2

This example is the same chord change, but now it's after two bars of the 'I' chord.

Example No. 3

Simpler variation on the 'F' chord.

Example No. 4

Here the same idea is used on the 'V' to 'IV' chord change.

Example No. 5

This example also happens on the 'V' to 'IV' chord change, but here it's different. Now it doesn't drop to the root of the 'F' chord but rather the fifth, in-fact it doesn't use the root note for the whole 'F' chord within that bar.

Combination One

With twelve-bar blues, the left-hand tends to be fairy simple most of the time, so here this drop is only used once, on the first chord change 'I' to 'IV' on bar two.

35 AUDIO

Combination Two

Here the drop at the chord change is used twice, in bars two and five with bar six mostly copying the previous bar.

36 ◀ AUDIO

Combination Three

This time the drop is used more often along with more variation within the pattern.

37 ◀ AUDIO

Different Octave Ranges

Don't forget that you aren't limited to a short range of motion, you can if you like play at different points on the keyboard, moving an octave lower or higher here and there. This example starts in a fairly standard position and then drops an octave for both the 'F' and 'G' chords.

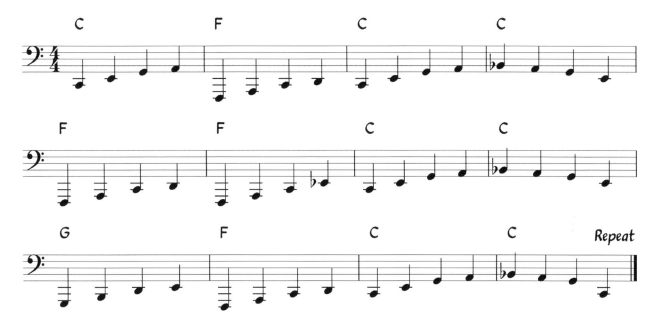

This example has the 'C' start on the lowest octave, the following chords being a mixture position wise, moving back and forth between octave ranges.

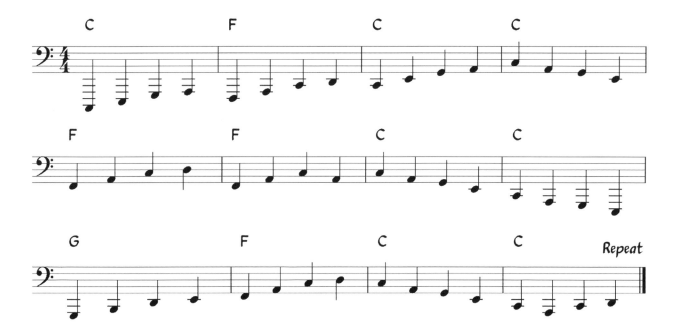

Alternating Root Patterns

Something else you can try is this, rather than walking the bass in an orderly fashion, you can jump or alternate the moving notes against a solid non-moving background, basically you alternate with the root note.

Example No. 1

Example No. 2

Example No. 3

Example No. 4

Example No. 5

These two combinations use a selection of patterns from the previous page, they do move around somewhat, but it's good practice to play around and get used to playing more complex patterns even if you don't use them often.

Combination One

38 ◀ AUDIO

Combination Two

39 ◀ AUDIO

Adding The Right-Hand

Once you have the basic idea of the walking-bass and can play through a chord progression with no problems, you will naturally want to add the right-hand. This all depends on your level of course, as you might already be happy playing over the top, but being a beginner style book we will go over a few basic ideas of doing this in an easy manner, to gradually incorporate the two together. Again, this is just a few examples of something simple to get started using both hands together if you aren't sure of what to do, so by all means do your own thing and disregard.

Example No. 1

The simplest way to begin is by just playing block chords at the start of every bar. This gets you using the right-hand but without having too much to think about. The 'I' chords use a sixth chord, the 'IV' and 'V' chords use a seventh chord.

Example No. 2

Here we still have the same chords starting at the beginning of each bar, but it also includes a repeat of the chord with a triplet feel pattern. The 'I' chords still use a sixth chord, the 'IV' and 'V' chords are seventh chords.

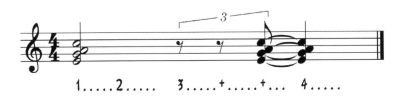

Example No. 3

Here the right-hand doesn't come in immediately but rather on the last triplet of beat one. This is followed by a one beat rest and a repeat of the chord for the remainder of the bar.

Example No. 4

This time we have a little pattern that starts with a major chord on the first beat, but then changes to a triplet feel on the second beat. After which we have a two bar rest giving the thing space to breath. Bars nine and ten take a break from this with block chords taking the patterns place, optional of course so play as you wish.

1.....   2....⁺....⁺...   3.....   4.....

Basic Guidelines

Okay then, we have looked at various ideas that can be used to create a walking bass-line on the piano, so now we'll put together some basic guidelines which can always be employed and are pretty much guaranteed to work.

Typical Bass Pattern Notes

As mentioned at the start of the book, the main notes or basis of the left-hand are as below. Obviously the actual notes will vary depending on which scale you are playing in, but the degrees of the major scale are universal.

ROOT	THIRD	FIFTH	SIXTH	OCTAVE ROOT

These are the basis of the left-hand, the root, third, fifth and sixth. The first three would form a major chord and obviously the sixth would create a major-sixth. These are the notes that you will use the most, and just these alone can create a perfectly usable walking bass pattern.

What Are Target Notes

These are the notes that you target or move towards when walking. A target note can in theory be any note at all (assuming that it works harmonically) but they most often the chord tones.

Root Notes

The root of a chord is the most important, as it defines the chord. So perhaps the main target note would be the root of the chord, which could be the chord you began with or a different chord on the following bar. So when walking you will often be thinking about and moving towards the root of the next chord.

Chord Tones

The other chord tones would be the next most likely targets, with the third, fifth, sixth and flat-seventh all being possible targets to end a pattern upon.

The Other Notes

As mentioned before, potentially any of the other notes could be used or considered a target as it's open to interpretation to some degree, but that's perhaps not something to consider beginning with, keep it simple.

Target Notes

The most likely target notes are the chord tones as shown below, being the root, third, fifth, sixth and flat-seventh.

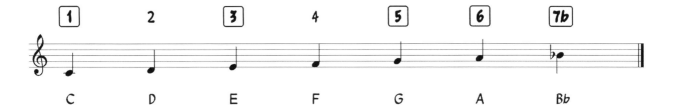

Pentatonic Scales

You may notice that these notes are all from the pentatonic scales, The root, third, fifth, and sixth from the major pentatonic and the flat-seventh from the minor pentatonic scale. So knowing your pentatonic scales in as many keys as possible might help you form the bass patterns.

Major Pentatonic

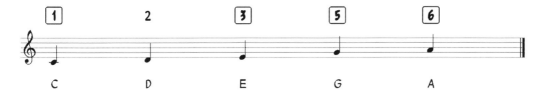

Minor Pentatonic

Quick Note

You don't necessarily have to think in this manner, the root note of the following chord will always be a target, but instead of considering target notes, simply memorise various patterns and combine them. This comes with practice but once you don't have to think about the music, that is when you know the music. How you approach this of course is up to you.

Passing Notes

This might seem unlikely, but pretty much any note beyond those listed as the basics are possible passing notes. At least at some point or other, as long as it works with the music, fitting the chords and using the non-chord tones in passing.

Definition

For our purposes here I will define a passing note as any note that is not a chord tone, instead being the notes that you will use between the chord tones.

Primary Passing Notes

Most notes will work most of the time, they won't work in isolation but rather when moving through them (often chromatically) and moving towards a chord tone or root note. I've initially omitted two of the possibles as they're tricky and best used in certain circumstances.

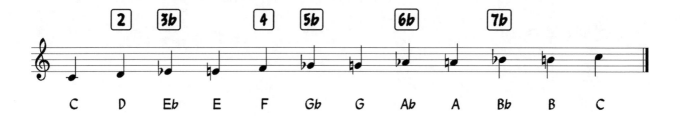

Secondary Passing Notes

These two notes I've listed separately. The flat-second is very dissonant, but you might (perhaps) use it when moving down to the root. The major-seventh also sounds slightly out of place but can be used when moving up to the root, or when walking down chromatically through a series of notes.

Chord Changes

When using passing notes in a bid to reach the root note of the next chord, the final note before that new chord can often be a semi-tone (occasionally a whole tone) above or below it. This was shown earlier regarding leading notes (a note that leads into the next chord) but these are also passing notes so some examples with this in mind will be good. Below are examples using notes above and below the target note for transitioning between chords.

Example No. 1

On the 'C' chord we move to the flat-fifth which is a semi-tone above the target note 'F' (being the root of the new chord).

Example No. 2

On the 'C' chord we drop down to the flat-fifth which is a semi-tone lower than the target note 'G' (being the root of the new chord).

Example No. 3

On the 'C' chord we move up and finish on the third, this is a semi-tone below the target note 'F' (being the root of the new chord).

Example No. 4

On the 'C' chord we move up over the two bars and finish on the seventh (unusually the major rather than minor) which is a semi-tone below the target note 'C' (being the root of the following chord).

Example No. 5

On the 'C' chord we move down and finish on the flat-sixth. This is a semi-tone above the target note 'G' (being the root of the new chord).

Example No. 6

On the 'G' chord we move up and finish on the fifth. This is two semi-tones (or a tone) above the target note 'C' (being the root of the new chord).

Example No. 7

On the 'C' chord we move to the fifth but then drop down an octave for a note which is a semi-tones above the target note 'F' in the next bar.

Further Passing Notes

There are obviously more passing notes available than just those that can be used to transition between chords, so here's examples that show passing notes in action.

Example No. 1

The 'C' chord uses the second (D) and flat-third (E♭) between the root and third before settling on the root of the next chord 'F'. The second and flat-third might be considered the passing notes as the others are chord tones.

Example No. 2

The 'C' chord is moving down from the fifth (G) and uses the fourth (A) and the second (D) as passing notes between the chord tones.

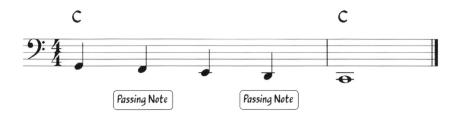

Example No. 3

The 'C' chord is moving through its chord tones (root, third, and fifth) and uses the fourth (F) and flat-fifth (G♭) as passing notes between the third (E) and fifth (G).

Example No. 4

Even though the sixth (A) can be used as a target note at times, here it is really used in a passing context to connect the chord tones together, bridging the gap between the fifth (G) and the flat-seventh (B♭).

Example No. 5

In the second bar we start with the fifth (G chord tone) before moving towards the root in the third bar. The three notes in-between could be considered passing notes. The sixth (A) and flat-seventh (B♭) could be considered chords tones, but here they aren't the targets they are simply being used to transition from the fifth (G) to the root (C). The major-seventh (B) is without doubt a passing note and not too commonly used, but it works here when moving between the flat-seventh and root.

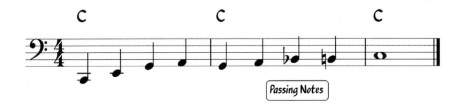

Example No. 6

This pattern moves around quite a lot, but in the first bar the flat-seventh could be considered a passing note as it is the sixth (A) that becomes the chord tone. In the second bar only the fifth (G) is a chord tone with the flat-fifth, fourth and flat-third all considered passing notes on the way to the root (C) on the third bar.

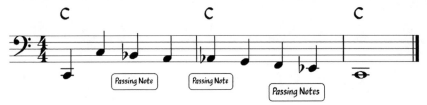

Fingering Ideas

Example No. 1

For a basic pattern (root, third, fifth, and sixth) this works perfectly, it's simple and comfortable.

Example No. 2

When moving further up (the root an octave up), people play this in various different ways, although to my mind one makes more sense than the others for a couple of reasons, but we'll go through some options.

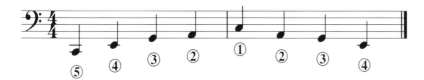

This is different from number one as it uses all five fingers (in order) as you move upwards. Now while this may seem a logical idea there are a few issues with this, it's rather awkward and cumbersome and leaves little room for further movements. I wouldn't play it like this.

Example No. 3

Here we cross over the thumb (1) to play the sixth with finger (2). This keeps the comfortable fingering from example one and allows the walk down to be a copy of moving up (simple). There's pros and cons to this.

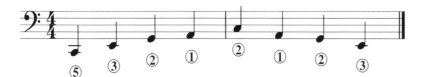

Example No. 4

Here we're moving up past the octave root, so we cross over the thumb again. This time we're using finger (3), which leaves us both (1) and (2) for further movement.

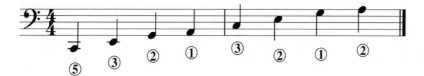

Example No. 5

In this example, when we run out of fingers on the sixth with the thumb (1), we simply move the thumb over to the root note and back down again to the sixth.

PROS – It's very simple, easy to remember and play.
It will work in every key (Important point).
Leaves fingers free to move either further upwards or back down again

CONS – It might feel like an unnatural movement to some people, depending on their background.

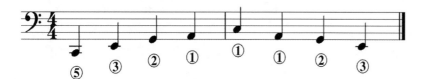

Example No. 6

Here you can see how using the thumb more can be beneficial, as this example has you drop back to the fifth in the first bar, leaving only the thumb available for the higher note.

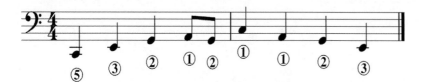

Example No. 7

This example has fingers (1) and (2) alternate at the end of bar one, going into bar two. After it drops down, finger (4) is used on both the two joining notes. This is a common technique within blues, dropping from a black note to a white with the same finger, it's a simple and smooth movement.

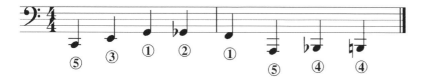

Example No. 8

This pattern is mostly chromatic with this being one example of how you could approach it. Finger (2) is used on two joining notes as it is dropping down from a black key to a white. This can't be replicated when moving back down, so it's using fingers (3) and (4).

Example No. 9

This is an alternative version that after the initial (5)(3)(1) repeats the (3)(2)(1) moving up and then repeats (1)(2) moving back down again.

NOTE

Dropping from a black key to a white with the same finger is dependent on the key and the resulting chords. What works in one key won't necessarily work in another due to the layout of the keyboard. The flat-third to third for example, it works for 'C' but not for 'D'.

Starting Finger Number

If you always start the walking bass on the root with finger number (5) and then use (3)(2)(1) on the following three notes moving up (a basic pattern), then the simplicity of this makes playing in different keys far easier. While some scales (depending on key) might sometimes require you to start with a different finger when beginning on a black key, here it just isn't the case.

Below we have the basic walking pattern (using root, third, fifth, and sixth). This is shown in 'C' and then in a selection of other keys/chords. Try them out using the same fingering numbers, you'll find that (5)(3)(2)(1) works everywhere.

Example In 'C'

Example In 'B♭'

Example In 'E♭'

Example In 'A'

Example In 'F♯'

IMPORTANT NOTE REGARDING FINGERING

You will have noticed from these examples that there is no absolute single way to play walking bass-lines, by its nature it evolves and so must the fingering.

Anything beyond the basic (root, third, fifth, sixth) pattern will require having to cross over the thumb or vice versa. Moving the fingers over the thumb or slipping the thumb underneath the fingers and so allowing the rest of the fingers to continue on. With the bass line potentially varying so much there's no set formula as such, but… One rule is that you ideally want the thumb to land on a white key, so the fingering will need to be ordered as such to work around this. As such, the thumb tends to be used after a black key moving upwards and before one moving downwards. Bear in mind that this is not always the case, but it's a good general rule. In certain keys/chords the thumb will be used on a black key for sure, but that's when the key/chord requires it.

Be Open And Adaptive

The best advice possible really is just to be open-minded and adaptive. There are some basic patterns that you may play for which you'll have a set fingering that makes sense, but once you go beyond this there are too many variations to always have a set fingering in mind. This is no bad thing, as with practice you will get used to improvising with the bass and the fingering to go with it. By just using a few basic ideas to stop the fingers becoming tangled, and having one free to reach for the next note, in time you won't even think about it.

Difference Between Blues/Jazz

This book is designed to help learn blues piano, but the walking bass is also very much a jazz thing, so what's the difference between the two?

Well they are kind of the same and yet also quite different. The basics are the same, it's more down to the differences in styles. Blues (and we are talking about traditional twelve bar blues here) tends to be played with a simpler pattern. The chord progressions and indeed the chords will tend to be simpler, but not only that, the left-hand will be more consistent, laying down a more repetitive pattern to which you can play over. Jazz (dependent on the actual variety) tends to be a little more complex, the chord progressions and left-hand patterns can (not always) be more involved, moving around a lot more than in a traditional blues piece.

Below is an example to explain what I mean. This is by no means an absolute, as styles of music mix/blend all the time, but you'll get the idea. A blues pattern tends to be simpler, being a solid background, the more jazz it becomes the more complex it can become, but as mentioned before, the two styles of music can overlap a lot.

Blues Type

A simple pattern that repeats with (for the most part) small changes here and there.

Jazz Type

Slightly more complex and less uniform in its structure, having more variation and chromatic movement between parts.

Different Chord Progressions 1

Now we are going to use what we have been covering but within a more complex chord progression. This is still very much a twelve-bar blues, but there are a few more changes than the basic standard progression.

Progression In Numerals

Some Example Keys

Key Of 'C'

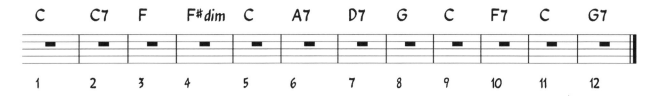

Key Of 'F'

Key Of 'G'

Combination One

This version has nothing overly fancy happening, which is more like the typical bass pattern you might use on a real blues piece, most of the time.

40 AUDIO

Combination Two

This version has more movement than combination one.

41 AUDIO

Different Chord Progression 2

This progression is a little different again. It's still a twelve-bar progression but this is now treading more into the jazz-blues territory, having more changes especially in the last two bars.

Progression In Numerals

Some Example Keys

Key Of 'C'

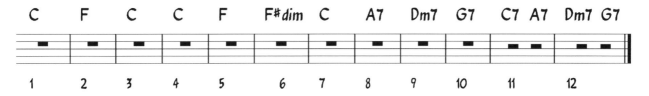

Key Of 'F'

Key Of 'G'

Combination One

This version has nothing overly fancy for the first half, but the later half has more movement, especially the last few bars with the extra chords.

Combination Two

This version has a little more movement earlier on, with the bass walking up from bar seven through to bar ten. This steps from one chord to the next, the root of each following chord targeted with a passing/joining note before it.

Practice Other Keys 1

Practice Other Keys 1

Key Of 'C'

Key Of 'D♭'

Key Of 'D'

Practice Other Keys 1

Practice Other Keys 1

Key Of 'F#'

Key Of 'G'

Key Of 'A♭'

Practice Other Keys 2

Key Of 'A'

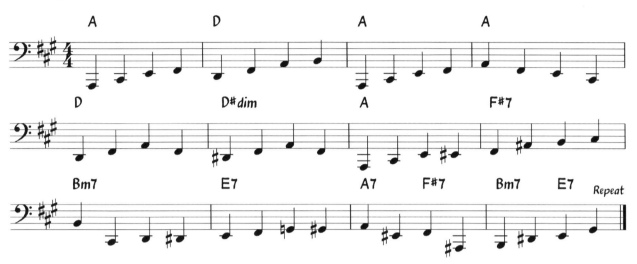

Key Of 'B♭'

Key Of 'B'

73

Practice Other Keys 2

Practice Other Keys 2

Key Of 'E♭'

Key Of 'E'

Key Of 'F'

Practice Other Keys 2

Playing In Octaves

Another way to play walking-bass on piano by using octaves, this produces a fuller/larger sound but isn't suitable for everything. The alternating octave style bass is more commonly used in boogie-woogie – often at quite a fair tempo – but it can also be used in a blues context and certainly jazz also.

Below are a few examples of alternating walking patterns. They might sound different to what we've already covered, but they are created exactly the same just with eighth notes alternating between octaves instead.

Example No. 1

Example No. 2

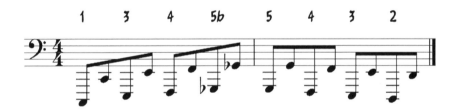

Example No. 3

Example No. 4

The alternating octave idea can be used on a lot of what has been covered, at least the ones that consist of quarter notes (crotchets). Because of this there is little point in going over all of them again (be it in octaves), but below are a couple of twelve-bars just to give some idea of what it's about.

Combination One

44 AUDIO

Combination Two

45 AUDIO

Non-Alternating Octaves

You can of course include octaves that aren't alternating, or combine the two ideas together to create something new and interesting.

Example No. 1

Example No. 2

Example No. 3

Example No. 4

Example No. 5

Example No. 6

What Next

So where do you go from here, how do you get better at playing this style of left-hand? There's two things that you really need to do and this applies to everything in music really, with every instrument and style.

Playing/Experimenting

You need to internalise everything you learn and this takes time and repetition. Once you can play something without much thought, only then do you truly know it, so time on your instrument/practice is everything.

Practice doesn't always have to be strict, as just spending time playing around for the fun of it is still helpful, it lets you discover what works and what doesn't and is really how improvisation begins.

Always remember that to truly improve you have to push yourself and try things that you can't actually do yet, or at least not properly. If trying to play something in a key you don't use very often is hurting your brain, then that's a sign that you are forcing yourself to learn something new, it's a good thing.

Listen Listen Listen

This is perhaps the single most important thing, listening to the music. Whatever it is you are trying to learn, whatever style it is you want to get into, it's vital that you listen to it, a lot.

By listening to the music you are internalising that sound and how it all works harmonically and rhythmically, you are taking it in at a subconscious level so that you already know what it is you are trying to re-create when you play, without that you are kinda flying blind.

There are two ways different ways of listening, you can listen in a casual manner while you are busy with something, working, reading or driving, which is fine and will certainly help, or… You can listen and really concentrate on the music, mentally analyzing what is going on and taking notes of what the artist is doing, this is a great way to teach yourself further. This can't be done all the time, but I would recommend taking the time to relax with the music you want to play and really take it in properly.

Transcribing

This goes much further than just listening, as perhaps the best way to learn is to listen to the music you like and copy it. The term transcribing refers to the act of writing down music, and if you wish to do that to go back to then that's fine. But rather than spending precious time doing that, just listen and work out the notes at the keyboard and learn what it is your favourite artist is playing. Many musicians mean this when they say that you should be transcribing, even if technically you're only doing half of the work, it's the learning part of the process that is important.

Learning by working out the music yourself benefits you in two ways. For one, it allows you to learn any music that you like rather than relying on someone having already transcribed to some sheet music or book. This really frees you, as although there's a lot of sheet music available these days, chances are there's plenty of music you'd like to learn that isn't available, so if you learn to do this yourself then you can learn from anything, any source and any song you wish.

Like everything else in life, this is a skill that takes time to learn, but you don't have to be a master at it to benefit. Take your time and work out what you can, as anything new will benefit you and in time you will get better and better. Plus, the music that you have transcribed/worked out yourself will stay with you far longer than something learnt from sheet-music, the process really implants the information far deeper and effectively than using sheet-music. I'm not knocking written music in any way, but don't rely solely on it, use every tool and method at your disposal to get the most benefit and learn at your best and most effective rate.

Downloadable Audio

Audio files based on the examples within the book are available to download from the website in MP3 format, simply follow the instructions below.

To access and download the MP3 audio files, simply visit the website…

www.tylermusic.co.uk

- Click on audio downloads
- Select the relevant book title
- Enter the password… **walking891**
- Click on the download icon

Once downloaded please save them for future use.

Also Available

Bite Sized Specifics – Blues Piano/Stride-Piano

Learn to play blues piano using the left-hand stride style. The second in a series that concentrates on a specific aspect of blues piano. Concentrating on the left-hand, it looks at what stride is and how it is created and various ways to which you can employ it in a blues environment.

Bite Sized Specifics – BluesPiano/Right-Hand Vol.1

Learn to play blues piano with the third in a series that concentrates on specific aspects of blues piano. Concentrating on the right-hand, it concentrates on the important aspect of comping, which is the more rhythmic side of blues with an emphasis on the important use of chords and repetitive patterns/riffs that form the backbone of the music.

Bite Sized Specifics – BluesPiano/Right-Hand Vol.2

Learn to play blues piano with the fourth in a series that concentrates on specific aspects of blues piano. Concentrating on the right-hand again, we look at how to play blues solos, for when the piano is the focal point of the music. Encompassing the riffs and licks used to create that timeless sound.

The Complete Blues Piano

The complete blues piano is a comprehensive guide to playing and improvising blues piano. It covers the fundamental principles of the blues and includes in-depth theory and techniques, along with example blues pieces to learn/study with downloadable audio. Ranging from fast boogie-type blues to slow blues, Chicago through to New Orleans, beginners to intermediate, this has it covered.

Piano Blues Scales

The ultimate guide to learning the blues scales for the piano. The scales are clearly shown and explained in all keys for both major and minor scales along with fingering suggestions. But it doesn't stop there, here we go further and include ideas like the combined scales and methods of how to practice and use the scales in a more musical and practical real world fashion.

Easy New-Orleans   For Beginners

Learn to play that unique style of blues piano from New Orleans, the style of Dr John, Professor Longhair and James Booker to name but a few. Covering everything from chord progressions and left-hand bass patterns and introducing the all important New-Orleans rhythm.

Easy Blues Piano   For Beginners

Learn to play blues piano with this beginners guide to for the piano. Starting out with easy examples, it starts with very basics of the blues giving a great introduction to the style to the new initiate. A fairly basic ability on the piano is of course required. With downloadable audio, start learning the blues today.

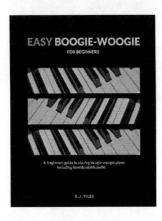

Easy Boogie-Woogie   For Beginners

Easy boogie-woogie takes the beginning boogie pianist through their first steps into the timeless style. It covers the basics with easy to understand clear explanations and includes example pieces throughout that start off easy and gradually increase in difficulty while adding extra elements. With downloadable audio,why not start learning boogie-woogie today.

Improvising Boogie-Woogie Vol. One

Learn to play boogie-woogie like the best of them. If you want to play boogie like Albert Ammons, Axel Zwingenberger or Jools Holland then this is the series for you. The first volume in a series of books to teach boogie-woogie piano, from the basics to more advanced techniques and everything in-between, this will give you the help and material you need.

Improvising Boogie-Woogie Vol. Two

The ultimate guide to playing boogie-woogie continues with volume-two, adding more left-hand patterns and right-hand riffs, including aspects like the walking-bass pattern, a little stride, rolling chords, using tenths and more complex rhythmic ideas.

Improvising Boogie-Woogie Vol. Three

The ultimate guide to playing boogie-woogie continues with volume-three, adding even more left-hand patterns and right-hand riffs to the series. Looking at the use of thirds and sixths, the use of scaler other chord progressions how such riffs are created and how to begin to create your own.

Improvising Boogie-Woogie: The Complete Edition

All three volumes in one edition. Available as perfect bound and spiral bound (spiral available through the website only). Learn to play boogie-woogie like the best of them. If you want to play boogie like Albert Ammons, Axel Zwingenberger or Jools Holland then this is the series for you. From the basics to more advanced techniques and everything in-between.

Improvising Boogie-Woogie: The Complete Edition

All three volumes in one edition. Available as perfect bound and spiral bound (spiral available through the website only). Learn to play boogie-woogie like the best of them. If you want to play boogie like Albert Ammons, Axel Zwingenberger or Jools Holland then this is the series for you. From the basics to more advanced techniques and everything in-between.

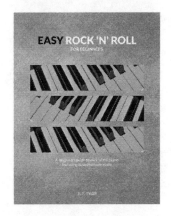

Easy Rock'N'Roll   For Beginners

Easy rock 'n' roll is for the beginner taking their first steps into the timeless sound of rock 'n' roll piano. Covering the basics with easy to understand clear explanations on how to play in the style of the likes of Jerry Lee Lewis and Little Richard. It includes example pieces throughout that start off easy and gradually increase in difficulty, while adding extra elements along the way. With downloadable audio

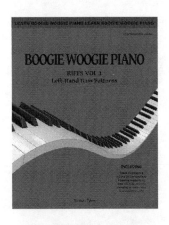

Boogie Woogie Piano: Riffs Vol.1
Left-hand bass-line patterns.
With sixty left-hand bass lines to master, including downloadable audio examples.
60 left-hand bass patterns
Fingering suggestions
Example 12-bar progressions
Downloadable audio examples of each pattern, at both full speed and half speed.

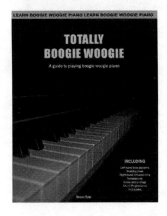

Totally Boogie-Woogie

This comprehensive book includes...
Basic structure and timing, left-hand bass patterns, walking bass, right-hand riffs, chords and scales.
Turnarounds and endings, and additional chapters on practising methods, transposing, along with plenty of general information and advice.

Tyler music.co.uk

For further piano books, sheet music and information on blues
and boogie-woogie music and events
visit the website at…

www.tylermusic.co.uk

Made in the USA
Columbia, SC
31 July 2024

39752484R10052